Application for Release from the Dream

Books by Tony Hoagland

Poetry
Application for Release from the Dream
Unincorporated Persons in the Late Honda Dynasty
What Narcissism Means to Me
Donkey Gospel
Sweet Ruin

Essays
Twenty Poems That Could Save America and Other Essays
Real Sofistikashun: Essays on Poetry and Craft

Application for Release from the Dream

poems

TONY HOAGLAND

Graywolf Press

This publication is made possible, in part, by the voters of Minnesota
through a Minnesota State Arts Board Operating Support grant, thanks
to a legislative appropriation from the arts and cultural heritage fund, and
through grants from the National Endowment for the Arts and the Wells Fargo
Foundation Minnesota. Significant support has also been provided by
Target, the McKnight Foundation, Amazon.com, and other generous
contributions from foundations, corporations, and individuals.
To these organizations and individuals we offer our heartfelt thanks.

Published by Graywolf Press
250 Third Avenue North, Suite 600
Minneapolis, Minnesota 55401

www.graywolfpress.org

Published in the United States of America

ISBN 978-1-55597-718-4

2 4 6 8 9 7 5 3 1
First Graywolf Printing, 2015

Library of Congress Control Number: 2015939972

Cover design: Kyle G. Hunter

Cover photo: Dan Fischer / Barcroft Media / Landov

for Kathleen Lee

Contents

MISUNDERSTANDINGS

THE EDGE OF THE FRAME

The experiment failed;
the lead did not change into gold.

But the alchemist remembered
the lute hidden in his closet.

—THOMAS OWENS

It is hard to drop from the self into the soul.

—JAMES HILLMAN

Application for Release from the Dream

A LITTLE CONSIDERATION

The Edge of the Frame

Joseph Cornell collected souvenirs of places he was miserable in,
which pretty much was everywhere he went.

Churchill felt afraid on stairs. Terrible migraines
of Virginia Woolf entered her skull and would not be evicted.

I read biographies because I want to know how people suffered
in the past; how they endured, and is it different, now, for us?

This bright but gentle morning, like the light of childhood;
then, because of the antidepressant, day by day,
                              the gradual return of curiosity.

What *is* a human being? What does it *mean?*
It seems a crucial thing to know, but no one does.

From my window, I can see the oak tree in whose shade
the man from UPS parks his van at noon
            to eat his lunch and read the ads for *Full Body Asian Massage.*

"You will conquer obstacles," that's what the fortune cookie said;
first I crumpled it up, then went back later to retrieve it from the trash.

Midnight, walking down Cerillos Avenue, alone,
past the auto dealerships and thrift stores,
                              past the vintage neon of the Geronimo Motel.

Someone's up late, painting the inside of Ernie's Pizza Parlor,
which will be opening in June.

As I walk by, all I can see
is the ladder, and two legs near the top, going out of sight.

Summer

The tourists are strolling down Alpine Street
hoping for a deal on hand-carved rocking chairs

or some bronze Kali Yuga earrings
from the local Yak Arts dealer.

It's summer. No one needs therapy for now,
or a guide to the aesthetics of collage

—laughing as they walk past the acupuncture clinic,
and Orleans Fish and Chips,

then double back to the Omega store
to look more closely at those shoes.

People like to buy. They just do.
They like the green tissue paper.

They like extracting the card from its tight
prophylactic sheath, handing it over,

and getting it back.
They like to swing the bag when they stroll away.

They like to stash the box in the car.
A forty-year-old man stares at a wetsuit on the rack:

Is it too late in life to dress up like a seal and surf?
—as the beech tree in front of the courthouse suddenly
                              fluffs itself up and flutters,

and a woman with a henna rinse
holds a small glass vase up to the light

to see the tiny turquoise bubbles trapped inside.
As a child she felt a secret just inside her skin,

always on the brink of bursting out.
Now the secret is on the outside,

and she is hunting it.

Ode to the Republic

It's going to be so great when America is just a second fiddle
and we stand on the sidelines and watch the big boys slug it out.

Old men reading the *Times* on benches in Central Park
                    will smile and say, "Let France take care of it."

Farmers in South Carolina will have bumper stickers that read
"One Nation, with Vegetables for All" and "USA:
                        Numero Uno for Triple-A Tomatoes!"

America, you big scary baby, didn't you know
            when you pounded your chest like that in public
                      it just embarrassed us?
When you lied to yourself on television,
                we looked down at our feet.

When your left hand turned into a claw,
            when you hammered the little country down
                and sang the Pledge of Allegiance,
I put on my new sunglasses
           and stared at the church across the street.

I thought I had to go down with you,
           hating myself in red, white, and blue,

learning to say "I'm sorry" in more and more foreign languages.

But now at last the end of our dynasty has arrived
            and I feel humble and calm and curiously free.

It's so good to be unimportant.
It's nice to sit on the shore of the Potomac
           and watch Time take back half of everything.

It's a relief to take the dog for a walk
           without frightening the neighbors.

My country, 'tis of thee I sing:
> There are worse things than being
>> second burrito,

minor player, ex-bigshot, former VIP, drinking decaf
> in the nursing home for downsized superpowers.

Like a Navajo wearing a cowboy hat, may you learn
> to handle history with irony.

May you gaze into the looking-glass and see your doubleness
> —old blue eyes in a surprised brown face.

May your women finally lay down
> the law: no more war on a school night.

May your shame be cushioned by the oldest chemotherapy:
> stage after stage of acceptance.

May someone learn to love you again.

May you sit on the porch with the other countries
> in the late afternoon,
>> and talk about chickens and rain.

Proportion

The attorney collects a fee of seven million
for getting eighteen million back

from the widow of the CEO
whose corporation stole three billion

from ten thousand
stockholders and employees.

She has to go down to one Mercedes
and take driving lessons.

The radio said expect delays,
but five thousand years for justice
                    still seems ridiculous.

What I heard from behind me at the baseball game:
"We can't see *anything* from here"—
                    it seemed so true of us.

The two young actresses flip a coin
to see who will get to play the cancer patient

because they know
the worst fate makes the best role

and that dying can be good for your career.

One of them will go to Hollywood and be a star.
The other will move to Cincinnati

and take photos of her twins
running back and forth through the sprinkler
                            in shorts,
soaking wet, shrieking with delight.

Application for Release from the Dream

This is my favorite kind of weather, this cloudy autumn-ness—
when long wool coats make shoplifting easy,

and you can see, in all the windows of the stores,
the nipples of the mannequins pushing through their warm cashmere.

I keep the wise books on my shelves, and take them down to read,
but I no longer believe in their power to transform.

What *is* it? Maybe all the mystery anyone could want
is trembling inside my abdomen already

like the fine tremble of the filament inside a bulb.

When I came to this place initially,
I thought I would never be able to bear
                                    the false laughter and the lies, hearing

the same stories told again and again
with the same inflection, in the same words.

But that is just an example of the kind of bad thoughts
                                    that sometimes visit me.

Ten years after being cheated by Jim, of Jim's Bookstore,
I still am angry, though I said nothing at the time.

Outside, a faint mist falling from the low, steel-colored sky
and the red light caught inside the strangely glowing trees.

"Thank you for the honesty of being afraid," I say to myself out loud,
                                    "afraid of things you do not understand."

Exhausted then, I fell asleep; but I awoke, knowing the rules.

If you aren't learning, you have not been paying attention.
If you have nothing to say, it is because your heart is closed.

Wine Dark Sea

"*Wine dark sea*—that's from Homer, you know,"
said my father, about a book that I was reading
called *The Wine Dark Sea.*

I was furious at the old idiot
for presuming that he might know something
I didn't already understand.

So I've grown up to be one of those people
who gets angry at trees
for behaving like trees,

who kneels in hotel rooms and bangs his head
softly against the carpet, asking for help,
another kind of room service.

I remember the time he told me he had read
Don Quixote in the original French.
When I wrecked the car it was him I called, collect.

At Christmas I'll send him a case of grapefruit.
When he dies, I'll fly to the funeral
with a whole unpublished text inside me,

which I'll quietly read en route,
making certain overdue corrections.
Looking out the window

at the Old World
passing below,
as dark and unknown as the sea.

The Hero's Journey

I remember the first time I looked at the spotless marble floor of a giant
    hotel lobby
and understood that someone had waxed and polished it all night

and that someone else had pushed his cart of cleaning supplies
down the long air-conditioned corridors of the Steinberg Building across
    the street

and emptied all two hundred and forty-three wastebaskets
        stopping now and then to scrape up chewing gum with a
           special flat-bladed tool
               he keeps in his back pocket.

It tempered my enthusiasm for *The Collected Letters of Henry James, Volume II*
and for Joseph Campbell's *Journey of the Hero,*

Chapter 5, "The Test," in which he describes how the
"tall and fair-complexioned" knight, Gawain,
           makes camp one night beside a cemetery

but cannot sleep for all the voices rising up from down below—

Let him stay out there a hundred nights,
           with his thin blanket and his cold armor and his
             useless sword,
until he understands exactly how
the glory of the protagonist is always paid for
           by a lot of minor characters.

In the morning he will wake and gallop back to safety;
he will hear his name embroidered into
           toasts and songs.

But now he knows
      there is a country he had not accounted for,
        and that country has its citizens:

the one-armed baker sweeping out his shop at 4 a.m.;

the prisoner sweating in his narrow cell;

and that woman in the nursing home,
     who has worked there for a thousand years,

taking away the bedpans,
lifting up and wiping off the soft heroic buttocks of Odysseus.

Special Problems in Vocabulary

There is no single particular noun
for the way a friendship,
stretched over time, grows thin,
then one day snaps with a popping sound.

No verb for accidentally
breaking a thing
while trying to get it open
—a marriage, for example.

No participial phrase for
losing a book
in the middle of reading it,
and therefore never learning the end.

There is no expression, in English, at least,
for avoiding the sight
of your own body in the mirror,
for disliking the touch

of the afternoon sun,
for walking into the flatlands and dust
that stretch out before you
after your adventures are done.

No adjective for gradually speaking less and less,
because you have stopped being able
to say the one thing that would
break your life loose from its grip.

Certainly no name that one can imagine
for the aspen tree outside the kitchen window,
its spade-shaped leaves

spinning on their stems,
working themselves into
a pale-green, vegetable blur.

No word for waking up one morning
and looking around,
because the mysterious spirit

that drives all things
seems to have returned,
and is on your side again.

Eventually the Topic

The reality TV show brought together fat white Alabama policemen
                            and African American families from Detroit
to live together on a custom-made plantation for a month.
America: stupidity plus enthusiasm is a special kind of genius.

"When I was a child," says Kevin, "I spoke as a child, and I thought as a
    child,
but now I am a man, and I have put away childish things."
His wife doesn't think that St. Paul was talking about giving up gluten.

The surgeons compare the human heart to an engine;
the car mechanics compare the engine to a heart.
The metaphor works for both of them,

and it explains why one of the mechanics, Carl,
has been asking the same woman out,
and being refused, for fourteen years.

This winter sky is flat, gray and stretches out forever,
a pure performance of the verb *to yearn.*

"Human beings weren't meant to live like this," said Aldous Huxley,
but what did he mean by *this?* and how do you define *meant?*

Eventually the topic turns out to be Time, Time and the self.
It's about getting tempered, like a sword held in the fire.
It's about getting cooked in the oven, like a loaf of bread.

One day when the smoke clears,
then, when that day comes, then—
we will use the sword to cut the bread.

Little Champion

When I get hopeless about human life,
which, to be frank, is far too difficult for me,
I try to remember that in the desert there is
a little butterfly that lives by drinking urine.

And when I have to take the bus to work on Saturday,
to spend an hour opening the mail,
deciding what to keep and throw away,
one piece at a time,

I think of the butterfly following its animal around,
through the morning and the night,
fluttering, weaving sideways through
the cactus and the rocks.

And when I have to meet all Tuesday afternoon
with the committee to discuss new by-laws,
or listen to the dinner guest exhaustively describe
his recipe for German beer,

or hear the scholar tell, again,
about her campaign to destroy, once and for all,
the vocabulary of heteronormativity,

I think of that tough little champion
with orange and black markings on its wings
resting in the shade beneath a ledge of rock
while its animal sleeps nearby;

and I see how the droplets hang and gleam among
the thorns and drab green leaves of desert plants
and how the butterfly alights and drinks from them
deeply, with a stillness of utter concentration.

DREAMHEART

Crazy Motherfucker Weather

Taking the car out of the rental parking lot,
almost getting fender-bendered by the guy in the BMW
speaking capitalist Cro-Magnon into his cell phone;

wondering whether the time has come
to get a gun;
already starting to look forward to my lethal injection—

Or I hang up the phone
in the middle of a conversation
at the moment it no longer interests me,

having reached some limit of what can be
reasonably endured—
What happens next?

Am I entering the season of tantrums and denunciations?
My crazy motherfucker weather?
Will I be yelling at strangers on the plane,

begging the radio for mercy,
hammering the video rental machine
to get my money back?

Knowing it a sin to waste
even a smidgen of this life
under the blue authentic glory of the sky;

wondering whether a third choice exists
between resignation and
going around the bend—

Yet still the wild imperative of self:
the sobbing sense that one has not been loved;
the absolute demand for nothing less

than transformation;
the flaring force of this thing we call identity
as if it were a message, a burning coal

one carries in one's mouth for sixty years,
for delivery
to whom, exactly; to where?

Dreamheart

They took the old heart out of your chest,
all blue and spoiled like a sick grapefruit,

the way you removed your first wife from your life,
and put a strong young blonde one in her place.

What happened to the old heart is unrecorded,
but the wife comes back sometimes in your dreams,

vengeful and berating, shrill, with a hairdo orange as flame,
like a mother who has forgotten that she loved you

more than anything. How impossible it is to tell
bravery from selfishness down here,

the leap of faith from a doomed attempt at flight.
What happened to the old heart is the scary part:

thrown into the trash, and never seen again,
but it persists. Now it's like a ghost,

with its bloated purple face,
moving through a world of ghosts

that's all of us—
dreaming we're alive, that we're in love forever.

The Roman Empire

The lady in the park ducks her head when passing me
and veers a little to one side to keep from touching me.

I understand. She only wants to get out of the park alive
with her aging, high-strung Boston terrier,

and I retract my flesh as much as possible
to let her by. We know,

each time a man and woman pass, each
time a man and woman pass each

time a man and woman pass
each other on an empty street,

it is an anniversary—
as if history was a cake made from layer after layer

of women's bodies, decorated with the purple, battered
faces of dead girls.

A visitor from outer space, observing us
from some hidden vantage place

would guess at some terrible historical event
of which our politeness is the evidence—

the man, attempting to look harmless;
the woman trying not to seem afraid.

Look at that dogwood tree flowering nearby, with a bird in it.

After you. No, after you.

But the Men

want back in:
all the Dougs and the Michaels, the Darnells, the Erics and Josés,
they're standing by the off-ramp of the interstate
holding up cardboard signs that say *WILL WORK FOR RELATIONSHIP.*

Their love-mobiles are dented and rusty.
Their Shaggin' Wagons are up on cinderblocks.
They're reading self-help books and practicing abstinence,
taking out Personals ads that say
      "Good listener would like to meet lesbian ladies,
                  for purposes of friendship only."

In short, they've changed their minds, the men:
they want another shot at the collaborative enterprise;
want to do fifty-fifty housework and childcare;
they want commitment-renewal weekends and couples therapy.

Because being a man was finally just too sad—
in spite of the perks, the lifetime membership benefits;
and it got old,
telling the joke about the hooker and the priest

at the company barbeque, remarking on the beer and
punching the shoulder of a bud
          in a little overflow of homosocial bonhomie.

Now they're ready to talk, really *talk* about their feelings.
In fact, they're ready to make you sick with revelations of
          their vulnerability—

A pool of testosterone is spreading from around their feet,
it's draining out of them like radiator fluid,
like history, like an experiment that failed.

So here they come, on their hands and knees, the men;
here they come. They're really beaten.
No tricks this time. No fine print.
Please, they're begging you. Look out.

Don't Tell Anyone

We had been married for six or seven years
when my wife, standing in the kitchen one afternoon, told me
that she screams underwater when she swims—

that, in fact, she has been screaming for years
into the blue, chlorinated water of the community pool
where she does laps every other day.

Buttering her toast, not as if she had been
concealing anything,
not as if I should consider myself

personally the cause of her screaming,
nor as if we should perform an act of therapy
right that minute on the kitchen table

—casually, she told me,
and I could see her turn her square face up
to take a gulp of oxygen,

then down again into the cold wet mask of the unconscious.
For all I know, maybe *everyone* is screaming silently
as they go through life,

politely keeping the big secret
that it is not all fun
to be ripped by the crooked beak

of something called *psychology,*
to be dipped down
again and again into time;

that the truest, most intimate
pleasure you can sometimes find
is the wet kiss

of your own pain.
There goes Kath, at one p.m., to swim her twenty-two laps
back and forth in the community pool.

—What discipline she has!
Twenty-two laps like twenty-two pages,
that will never be read by anyone.

Bible Study

Who would have imagined that I would have to go
a million miles away from the place where I was born
to find people who would love me?
And that I would go that distance and that I would find those people?

In the dream JoAnne was showing me how much arm to amputate
if your hand gets trapped in the gears of the machine;
if you acted fast, she said you could save everything above the wrist.
You want to keep a really sharp blade close by, she said.

Now I raise that hand to scratch one of those nasty little
scabs on the back of my head, and we sit outside and watch
the sun go down, inflamed as an appendicitis
over western Illinois—which then subsides and cools into a smooth gray sea.

Who knows, this might be the last good night of summer.
My broken nose is forming an idea of what's for supper.
Hard to believe that death is just around the corner.
What kind of idiot would think he even *had* a destiny?

I was on the road for so long by myself,
I took to reading motel bibles just for company.
Lying on the chintz bedspread before going to sleep,
still feeling the motion of the car inside my body,
I thought some wrongness in myself had made me that alone.

And God said, *You are worth more to me*
than one hundred sparrows.
And when I read that, I wept.
And God said, *Whom have I blessed more than I have blessed you?*

And I looked at the mini bar
and the bad abstract hotel art on the wall
and the dark TV set watching like a deacon.
And God said, *Survive. And carry my perfume among the perishing.*

Misunderstandings

I thought insulin was what they put in sleeping bags.

I probably should not have called my class in feminist literature *Books by Girls.*

When I compared humanity to a flower growing in the shadow of a
    munitions factory,
                    it may be that I was not being fair to flowers.

I thought someone was watching and keeping score.

I believed the desire for revenge was a fossil fuel that you could drive a
    lifetime on.

I thought suffering had something to be said for it.

I said, "Love me better or go to hell."
I said, "I will forgive when I am good and ready."
I said, "Rumors of my happiness have been greatly exaggerated."

I still don't understand why what I give and what I get back in return
                    never seem to weigh the same.

My favorite days were gray—troubled, moody, and infinite.

Each time I plunged into cold water, I was happy
in a way that can never be destroyed.

I went a million miles, I don't know why—maybe some kind of quest,
    maybe to hide.

All those years I kept trying and failing and trying
                  to find my one special talent in this life—
Why did it take me so long to figure out
                  that my special talent was trying?

Introduction to Matter

After I finally got over my sense of being a character in a book,

and the innocence had gradually drained out of me
                             through the holes life punctured in my container,

that's when I finally had time to stoop down

and look closely at the dry, exhausted-looking grass
next to the sidewalk, blowing back and forth all day,

and at the long cracked ridges in the asphalt parking lot
           shoved up from underneath by the oak nine feet away,

and at a puddle of water in the handicapped parking space
           exactly the color of the chocolate milk

we were served long ago in the grade-school cafeteria.

After I no longer believed I was a spy from another planet,
after I figured out that my imagination was not actually all that strong

—that's when I noticed the scruffy little circle
of stamped-out cigarette butts next to the hospital loading zone

where someone must have stood the night before

while looking speculatively up
at the spectral, green-blue foggy glow on the horizon, so beautiful

it might have been mistaken for the pulsing magnetic fields
                             of the rarely seen aurora borealis,

but was actually the municipality of Framingham, Massachusetts,
five miles to the north,

that never turns off its lights.

The Social Life of Water

All water is a part of other water.
Cloud talks to lake; mist
speaks quietly to creek.

Lake says something back to cloud,
and cloud listens.
No water is lonely water.

All water is a part of other water.
River rushes to reunite with ocean;
tree drinks rain and sweats out dew;
dew takes elevator into cloud;
cloud marries puddle;
                              puddle

has long conversation with lake about fjord;
fog sneaks up and murmurs insinuations to swamp;
swamp makes needs known to marshland.

Thunderstorm throws itself on estuary;
waterspout laughs at joke of frog pond.
All water understands.

All water understands.
Reservoir gathers information
for database of watershed.
Brook translates lake to waterfall.
Tide wrinkles its green forehead and then breaks through.
All water understands.

But you, you stand on the shore
of blue Lake Kieve in the evening
and listen, grieving
as something stirs and turns within you.

Not knowing why you linger in the dark.
Not able even to guess
from what you are excluded.

The Wetness

I wanted to write a simple poem
about the wetness between a woman's legs

and what kind of holy moment it is
when the man's hand quietly moves south

over the smooth curve of the belly
into the shade of that other hemisphere

and his fingertips find hidden in dark fur
the seam already expectant in its moistness.

I wanted to write about that moment
as if it was full of incense,

and monks holding up their Latin like a torch
deep inside a cavern of Gregorian chant,

but if I write that, someone will inevitably say what
                has that romantic foofaw got to do

with the beleaguered realities of love
or with the biological exigencies of lubrication

or with the vast, retarded hierarchies of human suffering?

And someone else will add
that the man's hand
represents the historical hunter-gatherer tradition

invading the valley of the woman's body
with the obsolete presumptions of possession,

whereas the woman's body is known to be
the starting place of agriculture,

doing just fine, thank you, by itself,

until the man's hand barges into her Shangri-La,
and tramples her zucchinis and tomatoes.

But to the man, the wetness is a blessing
for which there is no history;

a coin that cannot be counterfeit,

and when the man's fingers reach it,
the wetness ripples upward like a volt,
a cool wind, an annunciation

and he tastes it,
as if his hand was a tongue
he had sent ahead of him.

I wanted to write a poem about
                    the wetness
between a woman's legs,

but it got complicated in language.
It is a wetness the man would make for himself
                              if he could

—if he could only reach
                    that part of himself
which has been dry for years;

if he could only show
          a part of what he feels
                    when he finds out

he is not a thousand miles from home.
That he will not have to go

into the country of desire alone.

Romans

What a surprise, said Larry
when he heard that the L.A. police force had been accused
of beating their suspects for confessions;
What a surprise,
that they still have enthusiasm for their work.

He liked to say that all of us were Romans,
with our petty affairs and our corrupt politics,
our complex appetite for entertainment
and our far-flung, shaky empire.

It was spring in that city, and if you lived downtown,
you could tell the hour with your nose:
first the morning coffee exhaled by shops;
then the flowerstalls opening at ten;
then the lunch carts would start smoking sausage.

He loved the black lipstick of the young cashiers,
the portapotties and the video arcades,
the tourists lined up for the Holocaust Museum;
the rage that year for kiwi fruit.

In some parts of town it was said
you could buy a human kidney, or a heart.
Life was still life, after all:
it was stuffed full of interesting things.

Or you could head down to the east side
where the immigrant nannies were walking
the children of the rich,
murmuring together in Tagalog and French,
calling out a warning to young Witherspoon the Third.

Larry was on his third wife then,
or somewhere between the second and the third.
He believed in trial and error;
he believed in doing your best, and then giving up.

For him, we held a kind of distant beauty
based on our imminent extinction.
That was a Roman sun, shining on the duckpond.
Fluttering the trees, that breeze was Roman.

MISUNDERSTANDINGS

The Neglected Art of Description

The wind comes out of the east,
dips under the Verrazano Bridge,
and enters a corner of north Jersey,

brushing the storage tanks by the river
and the aging stucco of discount motels,
and the bodegas where they used to roll cigars.

Sometimes it gathers in a stand of elms
and seethes around in them,
bringing them to a boil, then just as suddenly

departs, flipping all the leaves up at once
like the skirt of a girl, to show
pale parts that never catch the sun.

How flimsy things are, and yet how real—
like the bunched-up roll of fat
revealed by the shirt of the grocery clerk

leaning over the soda supply,
as the low-slung jeans pull one way
and the shirt another—shocking, unbeautiful,

what the scholar from Yale would call
a "liminal area of embodiment,"
what her daughter would call "radical lard"—

but the art of description
is thrilled to reveal
what has not been noticed before.

Look at that electric-company technician
descending into a manhole on Dalzell Street
as if to remind us of the world

right underneath this one,
a mysterious place of cables and connections,
and subterranean tunnels,

where one might encounter the soul—
a place description has not been allowed to enter yet,
or rather, only allowed to go so far;

or rather, not permitted to say
what it has seen.

Airport

In the airport the fat sunburned people coming back from vacation
look happier than anyone, with their Hawaiian shirts and varicose veins
                              and faint aroma of suntan lotion.

I look down on them because their happiness is so superficial.
It is an imaginary battle that they win without trying,
                              by continuing to be themselves—

joking, telling family stories, eating nachos before lunch.
Like it or not, oneself is always the test case for the human condition.

The baby starts out as a luminous jellybean of god
and gradually transforms into a strange, lopsided growth:

a man who will not let himself be touched;
an aging girl who smiles and is angry with the moon.

Underneath the smile is bitterness, and underneath the bitterness is grief,
and underneath the grief the desire to survive at any cost.

The music on the airport intercom is supposed to make it easier.
That and the Southern accent of the flight announcers,

with their colorful speech impediments of moonshine and molasses.

"Where I am going I do not wish to go," wrote Bertolt Brecht,
but what he meant was that he did not want to be himself.

Yesterday I wished for rain, the cold clear kind that falls from very high,
and when it fell, I felt such joy.

But it's what I don't pray for that can rescue me.
Surprise, surprise, only surprise will help me on my way.

A History of High Heels

It's like God leaned down long ago and said,
to a woman who was just standing around,
"How would you like a pair of shoes
that shoves the backs of your feet up about four inches
so you balance always on your tiptoes

and your spine roller-coasters forward, then back,
so that even when you are spin-doctoring a corporate merger
or returning from your father's funeral in Florida,
your rump sticks out in a fertility announcement

and your chest is pushed out a little bit in front of you,
the way that majorettes precede a marching band?"

No, I shouldn't have said that—I'm sorry.
It's just my curdled bitterness talking; it's just
                         my disappointment flaring up
in a toxic blaze of misdirected scorn—

because today is one of those days when I am starting to suspect
that sex was just a wild-goose chase
in which I honk-honk-honked away
      three-quarters of my sweet, unconscious life.

Now my hair is gray, and I'm in the Philadelphia airport,
where women are still walking past me endlessly
with that *clickety-clack, clickety-clack,*
flipping their hair and licking their teeth,

while underneath my own shoes
I suddenly can feel the emptiness of space;
and over my head, I see light falling from the sky

that all these years
I might have been leaning back
to gaze at and long for and praise.

A Little Consideration

The rain washed some of the pollution out of the air,
and for a while, workmen with their shovels and their picks

stood in dry spots underneath the trees,
resting and smoking while the gutters dripped.

Just before the elections, and the roads are being paved
because the governor wants us to remember him in the dark of the voting
    booth.

In Hollywood this year I hear the girls are wearing four-and-five-inch heels,
driving the feminists crazy—some say in subservience to the patriarchal gaze,

some say in a renaissance of ancient foot-binding traditions.
The problem is that they feel beautiful—and how do you disagree with that?

I am thinking about this while on hold with the phone company, waiting
to talk to the person stationed like a punching bag at the gate of that major
    corporation.

Their power is to add a mysterious charge to my bill; *my* power
is to shout at their least powerful employee.

Maybe you're a very nice person, but you also want to be thanked for it.
Maybe you've memorized the names of your employer's kids, because
                        you think that you would like a raise—

So what? Just pay your bills on time, and spread a little flattery around.
Just set the mousetrap in the basement with a dab of peanut butter—
    the extra crunchy kind.

Big news flash: That's all that people really want these days.
That's as much as we aspire to. We don't need to be pampered, or lectured,
    or adored.

We're not goddamn babies anymore.
We just want to be manipulated with a little fucking consideration.

Please Don't

tell the flowers—they think
the sun loves them.
The grass is under the same
simple-minded impression

about the rain, the fog, the dew.
And when the wind blows,
it feels so good
they lose control of themselves

and swobtoggle wildly
around, bumping accidentally into their
slender neighbors.
Forgetful little lotus-eaters,

solar-powered
hydroholics, drawing nourishment up
through stems into their
thin green skin,

high on the expensive
chemistry of mitochondrial explosion,
believing that the dirt
loves them, the night, the stars—

reaching down a little deeper
with their pale albino roots,
all Dizzy
Gillespie with the utter
sufficiency of everything.

They don't imagine lawn
mowers, the four stomachs
of the cow, or human beings with boots
who stop to marvel

at their exquisite
flexibility and color.
They persist in their soft-headed

hallucination of happiness.
But please don't mention it.
Not yet. Tell me
what would you possibly gain

from being right?

Faulkner

Afterward, I tried to find the Faulkner story
                    where a man on horseback rides deep into the swamp
to find the Indians who are breeding runaway Negros

whose children they will sell as slaves
                    back to the same white man
from whom the parents ran away—

If I remember right, he wears a green-gray military cloak,
and knee-high leather boots
and he is singing a song about a girl he met in New Orleans
                                        named Lilly Malone,
as he passes under the giant parasitic orchids
that hang like milk-white lanterns from the trees.

I wanted just to sink
into the cool water of literature,
                    to drift and rest among the pages for a while

and not to think about my own life
                    crushed like an aluminum can,
                    where my wife was asking me to move out of our apartment,

weeping so hard she was difficult to understand,
                    because she didn't love me anymore,

and me flipping and flopping around inside myself
                    like a poor armadillo or raccoon that
doesn't know it has been hit by a car.

But I fell asleep among the boxes, and the open crates of books,
                    and dropped into a dream
where I was driving through a city in my old green van, looking for
                    the address of a guy I used to know

and when a policeman jumped out in the middle of the street
                         in an attempt to make me stop,
I ran right over him,
                         and just kept going,
hoping I had killed the stupid bastard.

That is what I learned from Faulkner: there is evil in the world
                         like a virus, or a lingering disease
that sleeps inside the rivers and the trees—

The reason for suffering isn't some bad choice you made,
                         or something you did wrong,

it isn't anybody's fault; it just exists,
it is a condition of this place;

and the only purpose that it serves
                         is that it wakes us up,
at certain moments in our lives, it rouses us

to get up on our feet and find the door.

Wasp

Why should I have to deal with so-called human beings
when I can be up on the roof
hammering shingles harder than necessary,

driving the sharp nails down
into the forehead of the house
like words I failed earlier to say?

And when a few wasps eddy up
from their hidden place beneath the eaves
to zoom in angry agitation near my face,

I just raise a canister of poison spray
and shoot them down without a thought.
Don't speak to me, please,
about clarity and proportionate response.

The world is a can of contents under pressure;
a human being should have a warning label on the side
that says, *Beware: Disorganized Narrative Inside;*
Prone to frequent sideways bursting

of one feeling through another
—to stare into the tangled midst of which
would make you as sick and dizzy as those wasps,

then leave you stranded on the roof
on a beautiful day in autumn
with a mouth full of nails,

trying to transplant pain
by hammering down-down-down
on a house full of echoes.

The Complex Sentence

The kind Italian driver of the bus to Rome
invited her to his house—she was obviously
hungry—and gave her sandwiches,
and raped her.

All those years ago: she smiles
while telling it—contemptuous,
somehow,
of her stupid younger self,

who still drags behind her like a can.
Grammar is great,
but who will write the sentence
to unpack her heart,

and how she thought her bad Italian
was at fault, and
how it took a year for her to say
the word for what had happened
                              in her head?

But that's why
we invented the complex sentence,
so we could stand at a distance,

and make adjustments
in the view
while trying hard to track
the twisty, ever-turning plot:

the loneliness of what we did;
the loneliness
        of what was done to us.

Controlled Substances

Look, they are burning marijuana on TV—
big green bales of it, trussed with official yellow rope;

doused with gasoline and flame,
                    flaring up in California light—

The Sheriff of Nottingham's men stand around
                    in their DEA windbreakers
arms crossed, in mirror shades,
expressionless—as if justice
                is required to be humorless.

See the black smoke rolling off in scarves,
the police dogs wearing strap-on air-filtration masks

so they won't get hooked
                and move to harder stuff.

Don't they know
that drab green vegetable
                is part of the country now?,

like Selma, Alabama, or Cesar Chavez, or Hollywood?
Why didn't they warn us
                about those other substances?
Like money,
        which teaches you to strangle time,

or the narcoleptic trance connected with a small lit screen?

Why aren't there TV ads with celebrity spokespersons
                who ask, in a concerned, grieving voice,
Does someone you love
              have an information problem?

Why don't they break down my door right now and arrest me
and send me to a rehabilitation program

for using sadness as a substitute for understanding?

The sadness that is an eventual, inevitable result
of not being able to understand anything.

White Writer

Obviously, it's a category I've been made aware of
$$\text{from time to time.}$$

It's been pointed out that my characters eat a lot of lightly braised asparagus
and get FedEx packages almost daily.

Yet I *dislike* being thought of as a white writer.

When I find my books in the White Literature section of the bookstore,
or when I get invited to speak on "The State of White Writing in America,"

dismay is what I feel—
I thought I was writing about more than that.

Tax refunds, Spanish lessons, premature ejaculation,
meatloaf and sitcoms; the fear of getting old.

I know that readers need to see their lives reflected on the page—
it lets them know they aren't alone.

The art it takes to make that kind of comfort
$$\text{is not something I look upon with scorn.}$$

But after a while, you start to feel like white
$$\text{is all you'll ever be.}$$

And gradually, after all the struggling against,
after tasting your own fear of being

only what you are,
you accept—

Then, with fresh determination, you lean forward again.
You write whiter and whiter.

Ship

At dawn I get up from my bed and draw the blinds;
the light through the bedroom window is too strong.
I don't want the sun entering my house so early
when the dreams inside my head are still wet paint

and part of me is still on board that ship I visit every night
that floats off shore—that ship whose crew and passengers
are girls—cabin after cabin, deck after deck, an ocean liner
full of women like a box of chocolates.

Tonight again I'll be there, trying to pry one of them
away from all the rest, into a pantry or a stateroom,
desiring fiercely to unwrap her with a kiss, whispering
to keep from being caught.

And it is perfect, I suppose. I am permitted to visit,
but not stay; that boat is not allowed
to come ashore, and wreck my life.
Night after night it sails through my interior, a monument

to immaturity, with its cargo of strange women
being smuggled through the grown-up world.
When I'm not there, I can imagine them:
playing cards in their pajamas, smoking cigarettes

and drinking wine; dancing with each other
to old jazz records on the phonograph—
laughing, and making fun of me, and all the other men
who visit them at night,

who think that women live out there, over the horizon.

Because It Is Houston,

the streetlights have to take the place
usually reserved for the moon in the poem,

and the traffic in the background with its roar and surge
stands in for the ocean
                           tossing wrecks like driftwood on the shore.

Because it is Houston,
the smooth little blonde talking on her cell phone

while backing her SUV at high speed through the parking lot
is a respected citizen

and the gnarled, serpentine, yearned-out limbs of oaks
above certain shady boulevards

suggest that even ugly can be beautiful.

Because it is Houston,
a moist wind blowing from the south at dawn

carries the faint petrochemical bouquet
                from the landfills of our fathers
                        and the landfills of their fathers.
How sweet it smells!

A morning shower
has knocked down blossoms from the honeysuckle bush
                              into the grass
like little ivory trumpets.

Because there is no one better qualified around,
        because it is Houston,

you are the one who gets to kneel
upon the buckled sidewalk

and look at them in silence.

Crossing Water

In late summer I swim across the lake to the stand of reeds
that grows calmly in the foot-deep water on the other side.

It is like going to a florist's shop
you have to take your clothes off to get to,

where nothing is for sale
and nothing on display

but some tall, vertical green spears,

and the small, already half-shriveled pale-purple blossoms
sprouted halfway up the sides of them.

Squatting softly in the cool, tea-colored water,
hearing my own breath move in and out,

leaning close to see the tattered, soft-edged
                                                    purses of the flowers,
with their downward hanging cones and coppery antennae.

—This is more tenderness than I had reason to expect
from this rude life in which I built

a wall around myself, in which I couldn't manage to repair
my cracked-up little heart.

Each time I make the trip, I get the strange idea that this
is what is waiting at the end of life—

long stalks slanting in the breeze, then straightening—
flowers, loose-petaled as memory, gray

as the aftertaste of grief.

Tonight, I'll lie in bed and feel the day exhaling me
as part of its long sigh into the dark,

knowing that I have no plan,
knowing that I have no chance of getting there.

I will remember how those flowers swayed and then held still
for me to look at them.

Update

So much depends
upon

a red multi-
corporation

glazed with
tax credits

beside the white
politicians.

THE EDGE OF THE FRAME

Reasons to Be Happy

Some birds are people-watchers.
The worms can hear us stomping over them.
The loaves and fishes multiplied the Christians.

We were wrong about so many things.
We thought the world was mute,
or dead, or just disinterested.

Yet the sunrise liked being looked at
by sleepy cabdrivers. The billboard
was unashamed of its Southern Comfort ad.

The night wind rustled
through the tops of cedar trees
standing all around a certain house

where worried people
lay in bed and listened.
What were the names

of those old Greek gods?
And where did they go?
Atlas—he's the one

who spent a long time
holding up
what did not belong to him.

December, with Antlers

Why are people wearing antlers in the hospital cafeteria?
Because it's Christmas, silly.

Can't you hear the sleighbells
drifting down like pesticide from all the hidden speakers?

Mr. Johansson says he doesn't get paid
      enough to wear a Santa hat,
but everybody else just goes along with it.

It's winter, the elevators ding, the stunned relatives get off and on.
If it is Indiana or Ohio, they bring food.

No one sees the drama of the not-dead flowers,
taken from the room of the deceased
and thrown onto the trash.

Was it Stevens, or Corinthians?—"We make our dwelling
on the slope of a volcano."

You have to admire the ones who stand outside to smoke,
studying the parking lot,
all James-Dean casual with their IV poles.

If you could see them through my eyes, they all have antlers.
Human beings are tough—

with their obesity, their chemo and their scars,
their courage in the face of dark prognosis.

Tough as Rudolf-fucking carcinoma.

Look. Here come the three wise women,
up the escalator, bearing Jell-O.

His Majesty

What does His Majesty Mr. Boombox-in-My-Jeep think
as he drives the beach road every night, at two a.m.,

under the bleached shell of the summer moon,
assaulting all the houses with his rude tunes?

Is that boom-boom-boom a cry for help? Is it
the kill song of a hunting shark, or

is that a neuro-limbic-node-blastoma I detect
spreading like junk food through the cheap

software of the American soul?

Atilla the Hun, in your combat-camouflaged new Jeep,
white boy pretending to be black, or underprivileged, or street,

driving slow enough to wreck the sleep of these
retired, pajama-wearing citizens,
                                        what is wrong with you?

I bet I'm not the only one to hope his vehicle might flip
at the zigzag bend of the canal

and toss him headfirst in the swamp,
                                        where the dreadlocked mangrove roots
will seek and suck the Rastafarian right out of him.

Oh peaceful, divine Florida night,
mesmeric waves shimmering with lunar light,

won't you rise up now and take your kingdom back?
Won't you inflict the human condition with a big flat tire

or write it a ticket for two thousand years
                                    of disturbing the peace?
Won't you make the little people all sit down for a minute

and listen to the spacious, frightening concert
of this living night?

Western

Here in this mountain vacation town, the bumper stickers say things like
    "Geologists Rock" and "Powder to the People"—

but those brown patches on the slopes mean that spruce trees
are dying in great numbers,
of a disease that hasn't been made public yet.

On the radio, you can hear salsa and mariachi—Spanish DJs
for the workers on construction sites,

short men in tool belts and Stetsons, with hawk-like Aztec noses
that have survived translation through twenty centuries, like twenty drownings.

All day, out of boomboxes on scaffolds, there are the *narcocorridas:*
"Hermanos de la Hierba," "The King of the Kilo,"
                  and "El Canto de Miguel Rodriguez,"

about the *vato* who made fools of the sheriffs, and brought in
          a ton of good shit
                    in the back of his Cadillac hearse.

Trumpets and a trampoline bass, cheerful but relentless, like angry laughter.

The scientists say the mountains are still rising, an inch or two every year,
                  taking the dying trees
with them toward heaven, higher and higher,

that most of us bipeds are doomed, but that no one should worry—
there's an endless supply of us here:

some still trying to have fun; some going downhill fast; some
trying to balance on the fence
               between irony and hope

looking around for a better position,
        even while admiring the toughness of these homo sapiens,

who seem capable of anything
        but changing the way that they think.

Song for Picking Up

Every time that something falls
someone is consigned to pick it up.

Every time it drops and rolls into a crack,
blows out the window of the car

or down onto the dirty restaurant floor
—a plastic bag, a paper clip, a cube of cheese from the buffet—

and there somebody goes, down upon their hands and knees.
What age are you when you learn that?

After Dante finished the *Inferno,* someone
cleaned up all the ink and crumpled paper.

After the surgeons are done with the operating room,
someone makes it spic and span again.

After World War One, the Super Bowl,
a night at the opera.

After the marching feet of all humanity
come the brooms and mops, the garbage men

and moms, the janitors.
One day you notice them.

After that, you understand.
After that, then, no more easy litter.

No more towels
upon the hotel bathroom floor. You bend over

for even tiny bits of paper;
or bitterly, you look back at your life—like Cain,

upon the body of his brother.

The Story of the Mexican Housekeeper

I had heard that one before, over the years—how some wealthy
                                  people in El Paso
hired a woman from across the border,

then kept her hostage for seven years
by filling her brown head with whispers of *la migra*—

and with their gringo cunning and average human greed
they had themselves a slave for minimum wage.

But when my father tells me the story, the name of the housekeeper
is Rosalina, and the rich bastards in El Paso

turn out to be Dave and Beth,
old family friends of ours—

and he still remembers the amazing enchiladas
she would bring in smiling on a big white plate on Friday nights.

A cloud slides over the sun, and I can see
the scabs and lesions on my father's scalp, the pink square shaped like Kansas

where the skin graft struggles like a crop to take.

I can see the slight tremble in his hand that holds the drink,
where the melting cubes are watering the Scotch.

Why does he bring up the story of the Mexican housekeeper?
And why does he tell it with a smile on his face,

like a naughty joke he is ashamed of liking,
but likes too much to keep it to himself?

Maybe for my father it is a story about how ignorant
a human being can be—how frightened, and cheap, how easy to deceive;

maybe for him it is a story of how some people
are just destined to be used by others.

Maybe he wants to teach me that again.

Or maybe he wants to get under my skin, to rile me up,
or make me ashamed of listening;

maybe he is giving me the story like a little cup of bile
to watch me struggle with the taste,

to see if I will spit it out and make a scene,
or bend my knee to him and gulp it down.

I sit there in my chair, sunk in fume and funk,
and here I grow afraid that the story of the Mexican housekeeper
                    is really about me—

someone paralyzed by life,
willing to take whatever I am given

in exchange for being safe, in my little room just off the kitchen,
with my ironing board and black-and-white TV.

Or maybe my father now is just a sinking ship, tilting and submerging, slowly
going down as memories drift up through his brain

like bubbles of exhausted oxygen,
escaping from his cargo holds and staterooms,

a multitude of stories all rising up in no particular order;
maybe the story of the Mexican housekeeper is just one of those?

But here she is, suddenly in front of us—
her brown face wrinkled after years immersed inside my father's mind,

it's Rosalina, making her return appearance,
wearing a dusty apron, holding a rolling pin in her left hand,

and she's tired, and scared, and she's mad as hell,
not at my dad, but me—yelling

that she doesn't want to be in this poem for one more minute,
and she's leaning right up into my face, spraying spit and broken English,

saying that I don't know nothing, *Nothing!* about her—
yelling that she wants to go back where she came from,

Please, Senor, she wants to go back NOW!

Coming and Going

My marriage ended in an airport parking lot—so long ago.
I was not wise enough to cry while looking for my car,

walking through the underground garage;
jets were roaring overhead, and if I had been wise

I would have looked up at those heavy-bellied cylinders,
and seen the wheelchairs and the frightened dogs inside,

the kidneys bedded in dry ice and Styrofoam containers.
I would have known that in synagogues and churches all over town

couples were gathering like flocks of geese
getting ready to take off, while here the jets were putting down

their gear, getting ready for the jolt, the giant tires
shrieking and scraping off two

long streaks of rubber molecules—
that might have been my wife and I, screaming in our fear.

It is a matter of amusement to me now,
me staggering around that underground garage,

trying to remember the color of my vehicle,
unable to recall that I had come by cab—

eventually gathering myself and going back inside,
quite matter-of-fact,

to collect the luggage
I would be carrying for the rest of my life.

Real Estate

Outside the new apartment complex,
they raised a giant sign that says *FREE RENT;*
beside the *FREE,* they placed a little asterisk.

On the train, people looking down into their gadgets.
It's not the end of the world.
It's only the twenty-first century.

"To thine own self be true: I drive the new sedan from BMW."
"I will not fear my freedom: I wear
the new cashmere from Eileen Fisher."
Also a men's cologne from Calvin Klein called *Justice for All.*

I suppose *evil* is too strong a word.
I know the term *zombie* lacks a sense of proportion.
I don't believe irony will correct the situation.
But I will not say it is alright with me.

"Bombing that city was a terrible mistake,"
the four-star general says on television,
"but it taught me a lot about myself."
Maybe he should give a medal to his therapist.

And they drag us into shallower and shallower waters.
They take what is dearest to us and use it as bait.
They turn our wishes into merchandise.

When I found out, almost by accident,
that I had inherited the world
—that it was precious, that I was
responsible for keeping it safe—

Well, imagine how embarrassing it would be for *you*
to admit that you had been asleep;
that somehow, while you were not paying attention,

someone had acquired the rights for the trees
and the beaches and hills
and exclusive use of all the creatures of the sea.

While you were watching the pretty pictures,
and drinking a perfectly innocent Pepsi-Cola
—your world, and that of your children

and their children, and the beasts of the fields,
and the green, green Earth itself,
had been stolen.

Fetch

Who knew that the sweetest pleasure of my fifty-eighth year
would turn out to be my friendship with the dog?

That his trembling, bowlegged bliss at seeing me stand there with the leash
would give me a feeling I had sought throughout my life?

Now I understand those old ladies walking
their Chihuahuas in the dusk, plastic bag wrapped around one hand,

content with a companionship that, whatever
else you think of it, is totally reliable.

And in the evening, at cocktail hour,
I think tenderly of them

in all of those apartments on the fourteenth floor
holding out a little hotdog on a toothpick

to bestow a luxury on a friend
who knows more about uncomplicated pleasure

than any famous lobbyist for the mortal condition.
These barricades and bulwarks against human loneliness,

they used to fill me with disdain,
but that was before I found out my metaphysical needs
                                        could be so easily met

by the wet gaze of a brown-and-white retriever
with a slight infection of the outer ear
                        and a tail like a windshield wiper.

I did not guess that love would be returned to me
as simply as a stick returned when it was thrown

again and again and again—
in fact, I still don't exactly comprehend.

What could that possibly have to teach me
about being human?

Summer Dusk

I put in my goddamn hearing aid
in order to listen to a bird that sounds
like the side of a drinking glass
struck lightly by a fork

and try not to hate a life
that dips you in time like a teabag
over and over and pulls you up
each year a slightly different color.

Yet I like this hour when the air goes soft
and leaves stir with relief at the end
of their labor of being leaves.
"What a piece of work is man," I say,

not knowing Hamlet said it first—
"how noble in reason, how infinite in faculties,
in form and moving how express; in apprehension how like an angel,
and yet, to me, the quintessence of dust!"

This hour of the evening
with a little infinity inside,
like an amnesty from the interminable
condition of being oneself.

This half-hour when you look out
and see that it is sweet.
Even in my deafness I can hear
the bird whose name I do not know

speaking to someone in the dusk.

There Is No Word

There isn't a word for walking out of the grocery store
with a gallon jug of milk in a plastic sack
that should have been bagged in double layers

—so that before you are even out the door
you feel the weight of the jug dragging
the bag down, stretching the thin

plastic handles longer and longer
and you know it's only a matter of time until
the strap breaks or the bottom suddenly splits
and spills its contents to the ground.

There is no single, unimpeachably precise word
for that vague sensation of something
moving away from you
as it exceeds its elastic capacity

which is too bad because that is the word
I would like to use to describe
standing on the street and chatting with a friend,

as the awareness gradually dawns on me that he
is no longer a friend,
but only an acquaintance

—until this moment as we say good-bye,
when I think we share a feeling of relief,
an unspoken recognition

that we have reached the end of a pretense
—though to tell the truth,
what I already am thinking

is that language deserves the credit—
how it will stretch just so much and no further;
how there are some holes it will not cover up;

how it will move, if not inside, then
around the circumference
of almost anything—

how, over the years, it has given me back
all the hours and days, all the
plodding love and faith, all the

misunderstandings and secrets and mistakes
I have willingly poured into it.

Aubade

The moon is going down, innocent and pale as a wafer
dissolving in the mouth of a Catholic,

and those first, high-flying birds of dawn
are only faintly visible, like an image developing.

Just off stage, the rooster someone keeps illegally
in the city crows its magnificent cry,

blessing, who knows, maybe the child
just conceived inside a woman's body.

Such tranquility—the neighbors haven't started fighting
yet, nor their loud hyena laughter.

It's peaceful as a golf course in Jerusalem,
remembering when it used to be a meadow.

And we still love each other, in a way that makes us
tolerant, alert, perhaps a little vain

but also, we are getting older.
Come over here, darling,

and put your hand on my head
and tell me if you think this is a tumor.

Note to Reality

Without even knowing it, I have
                believed in you for a long time.

When I looked at my blood under a microscope
I could see the truth multiplying itself over and over.

It was not sirens, nor history books, nor stage-three lymphoma
                that at last persuaded me,

but your honeycombs and beetles; the dry blond fascicles of grass
                thrust up above the January snow.

When my friend died on the way to the hospital,
                it was not his death that so astounded me,

but that the driver of the cab
         did not insist upon the fare.

Quotation marks: I don't know what to put inside them.
Shall I say that "I" "have been hurt" by "you"?

I speak now because experience has shown me
                that my mind will never be clear for long

and I have given up
on getting back to the sky where I started.

I am as thick-skinned and selfish and male, as jealous and afraid
         as I have ever been.

I float on your surface; your nets and tides entangle me.

The breeze so cool today, the sky is smeared with bluish grays and whites.

The parade for the slain police officer
goes past the bakery,

and the smell of fresh bread
makes the mourners salivate against their will.

Acknowledgments

Thanks to the editors of the magazines in which these poems first appeared:

The American Poetry Review: "Aubade," "The History of High Heels,"
"The Edge of the Frame," "Application for Release from the Dream," "There
Is No Word," "Misunderstandings," "The Wetness"

The Cortland Review: "His Majesty"

Green Mountains Review: "Western," "Proportion," "Controlled Substances,"
"The Neglected Art of Description"

The New Ohio Review: "Ode to the Republic," "Fetch," "The Story of the
Mexican Housekeeper"

The New Yorker: "The Hero's Journey"

Orion: "Reasons to Be Happy"

The Paris Review: "White Writer"

Ploughshares: "December, with Antlers," "Faulkner," "Introduction to Matter"

Poetry: "Summer," "Don't Tell Anyone," "Bible Story," "Note to Reality"

Poetry Daily: "Coming and Going"

Southern Mississippi Review: "Real Estate"

The Sun: "The Social Life of Water," "Summer Dusk," "Little Champion,"
"Ship," "Please Don't," "Special Problems in Vocabulary," "Song for
Picking Up"

The Threepenny Review: "Wine Dark Sea"

Tin House: "The Roman Empire," "Crazy Motherfucker Weather,"
"Dreamheart"

"White Writer" also appeared in *The Best American Poetry 2014,* edited by Terrance Hayes and David Lehman, and published by Scribner.

I owe special thanks to the friends and colleagues who have helped me write and revise these poems: foremost, Ken Hart and Kathleen Lee, and the poets of my Santa Fe writing group: Joanne Dwyer, Elizabeth Jacobson, and Rob Wilder. In addition, Carl Dennis and Peter Harris have helped me many times with their readings and encouragement. Finally, I thank Jeff Shotts for his always-meticulous readings and thoughtful responses.

TONY HOAGLAND is the author of four previous collections of poetry, including *Unincorporated Persons in the Late Honda Dynasty* and *What Narcissism Means to Me*, a finalist for the National Book Critics Circle Award. He has received the Jackson Poetry Prize from Poets & Writers, the Mark Twain Award from the Poetry Foundation, and the O. B. Hardison, Jr. Poetry Prize from the Folger Shakespeare Library. He teaches at the University of Houston and in the low-residency MFA program at Warren Wilson College. He lives in Santa Fe, New Mexico.

The text of *Application for Release from the Dream* is set in Utopia.
Book design by Rachel Holscher.
Composition by BookMobile Design and Publishing Services,
Minneapolis, Minnesota.
Manufactured by Versa Press on acid-free,
30 percent postconsumer wastepaper.